11/02

The
War
in the
Trenches

Ole Steen Hansen

RAINTREE
STECK-VAUGHN
PUBLISHERS

A Harcourt Company

Austin   New York
www.steck-vaughn.com

THE WORLD WARS

Published by Raintree Steck-Vaughn Publishers,
an imprint of Steck-Vaughn Company

Library of Congress Cataloging-in-Publication Data
Hansen, Ole Steen.
The war in the trenches / Ole Steen Hansen.
    p.   cm.—(The World Wars)
    Includes bibliographical references and index.
    ISBN 0-7398-2752-9
    1. World War, 1914–1918—Juvenile literature.
    [1. World War, 1914–1918. 2. World War, 1914–1918—
    Trench warfare. 3. World War, 1914–1918—Campaigns—
    Western front.]
    I. Title. II. Series.
    D522.7.H36   2000
    940.3—dc21   00-027840

Printed in Italy. Bound in the United States.
1 2 3 4 5 6 7 8 9 0 05 04 03 02 01

Cover photographs:
Attacking on the Somme (Topham Picturepoint);
World War I medals (Peter Newark's Military Pictures)

Picture acknowledgments
AKG London 8, 9 (top), 9 (bottom), 11, 12, 13, 20, 29 (bottom), 36, 37, 38, 43, 46, 57, 59; Mary Evans Picture Library 4; The Hulton Getty Picture Collection 42, 51 (bottom); John Malam 22 (top), 28, 54; Peter Newark's Military Pictures 7, 14, 15, 16 (top), 17, 19, 23, 25, 26, 32, 49 (bottom), 35, 40, 44, 55, 58; Popperfoto 5, 21, 22 (bottom), 31, 37, 45, 48, 56; Hodder/Wayland Picture Library 10, 16 (bottom), 24, 27, 29 (top), 30, 32 (top), 33, 34, 41, 51, 52, 53 (top), 53 (bottom).

Contents

Origins of World War I

The 19-year-old student Gavrilo Princip couldn't believe his luck. Together with five other young Serbs, he had gone to Sarajevo in Bosnia on June 28, 1914. Their purpose was to kill the visiting Austro-Hungarian Archduke Franz Ferdinand. The six men were hardly cold-blooded terrorists. Rather, they could be described as romantic nationalists trying to free Bosnia from Austro-Hungarian rule. Early on, their plan had not met

An artist's impression of the assassination in Sarajevo, published in the magazine Le Petit Journal.

Gavrilo Princip, whose actions in Sarajevo sparked the chain of events leading to World War I.

with success. One had gone home feeling sorry for the archduke and his wife, and one had thrown a bomb and missed. Now the archduke's car took a wrong turn and stopped briefly just where Gavrilo, by chance, had positioned himself with a gun. Nothing was easier than to jump onto the running board of the car—shooting from such a close distance he couldn't miss. The archduke and his wife died shortly afterward. Gavrilo Princip was arrested immediately. Due to his youth he was sentenced to only 20 years in prison. However he died of tuberculosis in 1918.

The assassination in Sarajevo triggered events that soon led to all the major powers of Europe going to war with one another. Even though Europe was shocked by the killing, it is difficult to see why the death of just two people should lead to the deaths of millions of others.

To understand why, it is necessary to look beyond Sarajevo.

European domination

At the beginning of the twentieth century, the world was dominated by Europe. Great Britain and France both ruled large empires. Russia had expanded its territory to include all of Siberia. Austria-Hungary had a population larger than that of either Great Britain or France. It was made up of Austrians, Magyars from Hungary, and several other ethnic groups, including the peoples of Bosnia, who had come under the rule of Austria-Hungary in 1878.

For centuries Central Europe had been a patchwork of small German states. During the second half of the nineteenth century, these states had been combined to form a united Germany dominated by the state of Prussia. Germany was well on its way to becoming Europe's leading industrial power.

Country	Population (millions)
Austria-Hungary	51
France	37
Germany	67
Russia	164
United Kingdom	46

Steel production (millions of tons)		
Country	1890	1910
Austria-Hungary	0.5	2.2
France	0.7	3.4
Germany	2.3	13.8
Russia	0.4	3.5
United Kingdom	3.6	5.9

Source: A.J.P. Taylor, *The Struggle for Mastery in Europe, 1848–1918*

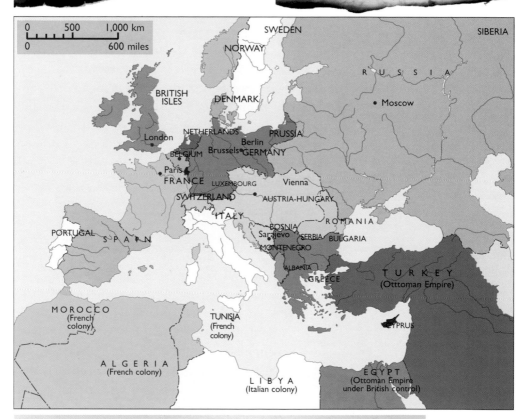

Military strength in 1914 (millions of men)			
Country	Peacetime strength	Men of military age	percent trained
Austria-Hungary	0.478	6.12	49
France	0.827	5.94	85
Germany	0.761	9.75	50
Russia	1.445	17.00	35
United Kingdom	0.248	6.43	4–8

Source: N. Ferguson, *The Pity of War*

Political map of Europe and North Africa in 1914. World War I would completely change many of the borders shown here.

The years leading up to 1914 were an exciting time in Europe. Progress in industry and technology helped create wealth on a scale never seen before. Airplanes and airships excited everybody—it seemed that only the sky was the limit to what people could do! Already, two million private cars had been produced worldwide. However, luxuries such as cars remained a privilege of the rich—the cost of a Renault amounted to eight years' worth of a French industrial worker's wages.

This 1912 motor car advertisement illustrates the fascination with modern inventions such as cars and airplanes that was typical of the years leading up to World War I.

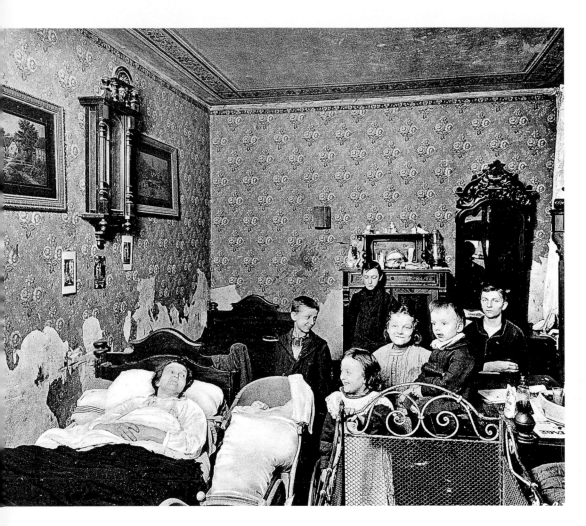

Many working-class families shared a single room among them, like this German family living in Berlin in 1913.

Antimilitarism

Wealth was anything but equally shared. Most people belonged to the working class. They lived poor lives, with families sharing perhaps just one room in a slum dwelling and spending most of their income on food. The upper classes and middle classes, on the other hand, were enjoying the new revolution in industry and technology. They could afford the products of industry, they could travel on trains and ships, and they could even buy recently introduced exotic fruits like bananas. This comfortable life would clearly be upset if war broke out. Many dreaded the idea of a major war in Europe. Making more money through foreign investments seemed a much better prospect for the future.

For political reasons, many working-class people were also against preparing for war. In England the Labour Party was anti-militarist and viewed the talk of war as propaganda; this allowed the "merchants of death" (arms manufacturers) to make money from their arms industries. In Germany, the social democrats in the SPD (*Sozialdemokratische Partei Deutschlands*) were strongly antimilitarist. Karl Liebknecht of the SPD claimed that militarism was "supporting capitalism against the struggle of the working class for freedom." The SPD got 34.8 percent of the vote in 1912, whereas the National Liberals—advocates of an aggressive foreign policy and increased spending on arms—got only 13.6 percent.

As the countries of Europe grew richer, more people could afford luxuries such as vacations at beach resorts.

Karl Liebknecht at a rally in Berlin. He spoke out strongly against militarism.

Fear of attack

Even if war was not desired, it was nonetheless expected. All the major powers had fought each other before at various times through history. In the nineteenth century, nationalism had swept through Europe. People began to think of themselves as Germans, Russians, or French. Everybody felt superior to other nations, and everybody assumed that the others might attack if they grew too strong. Had world history not proved again and again that if a country were strong it would attack another sooner or later?

The fear of attack was fueled by strongly nationalist publications. British books like *The Invasion of 1910* pictured a German army invading Great Britain, ultimately to be destroyed. The opposite story was found in the German book *Sink, Burn, Destroy: The Blow Against*

Fervent national pride affected all ages, including these boys from England's Eton School, shown parading with their rifles.

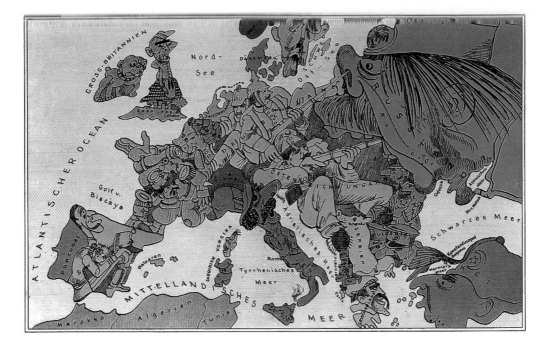

Nationalism gave rise to many satirical cartoons showing other nations as in the wrong. However, some artists chose to satirize the entire political situation. This cartoon shows the complex tensions and fears existing in Europe in 1914.

Germany, in which British soldiers were the "bad guys." Some authors took a more satirical stand. In a series of British cartoons, invading Germans attacked the beach at Yarmouth dressed in bathing costumes.

The countries of Europe tried to make their position as strong as possible against the threat of war. One way to do this was to form alliances. Russia, France, and Great Britain agreed to support one another. Germany similarly joined with Austria-Hungary. Not everybody agreed with these alliances. Relations among Russia, France, and Great Britain had often been poor in the nineteenth century, and many English people saw themselves as culturally closer to the "civilized Germans" than to the "barbaric Russians." For Great Britain, though, an alliance with Russia and France seemed to be a way to avoid conflict with these colonial powers.

Expectations of war led to an arms race. From 1894 to 1914, Great Britain increased its spending on arms by 117 percent, France by 92 percent, and Germany by 158 percent. The countries of Europe drew up detailed plans of action in the event of war, but none were more detailed than that of Germany, which expected a war with both Russia and France. The German emperor, Kaiser Wilhelm II, firmly believed that Russia and France would attack, and that the solution was for Germany to strike first. Alfred von Schlieffen, the chief of the German general staff, had in 1905 planned how to deal with the problem of fighting on two fronts. Marching through Belgium first, the German army would knock out France with a single, fast blow. Russia was seen as the more formidable enemy, but was likely to be slower to mobilize its vast army. Hence, after victory over France, the German army would be transferred by train to the Eastern Front. The "Schlieffen plan" relied on carefully prepared train schedules and speed. It would take 11,000 trains to move two million men and 600,000 horses to the front in just 13 days.

The crisis escalates

In the Balkans, nationalism had created an unstable situation. Several minor wars had been fought as the century-old dominance of the Ottoman Empire diminished. The Balkan wars (1912–13) left Serbia in a strong position. Austria-Hungary used the assassination in Sarajevo as a reason to declare war on Serbia on July 28, in order to limit Serbian influence. Russia felt obliged to help Serbia and started to mobilize its army. At the time, mobilization was seen as a diplomatic tool —in this case a way to put pressure on Austria-Hungary. Russia did not necessarily expect actually to go to war.

A German army unit preparing to leave for the front. Trains were indispensable to the armies in World War I.

Thinking war to be inevitable and using the logic of the Schlieffen plan, the leadership in Germany declared war on both Russia and France. When the German army marched into Belgium, Great Britain declared war on Germany. There could be no turning back now. The railroads that had helped to create an industrialized Europe now took millions of young men to the war front in accordance with carefully prepared timetables.

German soldiers in Brussels on August 20, 1914. The German invasion of Belgium caused Great Britain to declare war on Germany.

Thus a killing in Sarajevo plunged Europe into war. The war might have happened in any case due to some other cause. Or it might not have occurred. The irony is that all the major powers went to war in order to defend themselves, and all believed in the righteousness of their cause. Seen in this light, the outbreak of World War I in 1914 is one of the greatest tragedies in history.

1914: A New Kind of War

"The spade will be as indispensable to a soldier as his rifle. The first thing every man will have to do, if he cares for his life at all, will be to dig a hole in the ground." Ivan Bloch, a banker living in Warsaw under Russian rule, wrote these prophetic words in his book *Is War Now Impossible?*, published in 1899. He assumed that the new quick-firing weapons would destroy any possibility of successful attack. Bloch had made a remarkably accurate prediction of what was about to happen in World War I. His books were translated into several languages, but they had little impact on the thinking of military leaders.

The weapons available to soldiers at the beginning of World War I were far more lethal than those used by armies during the nineteenth century. Here a private from the British Devonshire Regiment is armed with a magazine rifle.

The scramble for action

The armies that went to war in August 1914 were led by generals with a strong faith in the power of the attack. However, the more perceptive ones knew that relatively recent, if smaller, wars such as the Russo-Japanese war of 1904–1905, had already illustrated the changing nature of warfare. In the nineteenth century (for example, during the Civil War) an infantryman could deliver 1 to 2 shots per minute at an effective range of up to 650 ft. (200 m). By 1914 soldiers could shoot up to 15 rounds per minute at ranges several times longer. A single machine gun could fire bullets faster and over a wider area than hundreds of riflemen could decades before.

Despite this, thoughts of victory rather than casualties were in the minds of most people in August 1914. Anti-militarist voices trying to point out the futility of the war were drowned by the waves of nationalistic enthusiasm sweeping over Europe. In most countries men were drafted, but many more volunteered, afraid to miss the action. Great Britain had only a small professional army and started to raise a new army of volunteers. In Belgium, the German army behaved ruthlessly to suppress opposition from the local population. These atrocities were wildly exaggerated in the British and French press, encouraging even more men to volunteer.

Machine guns such as this one were destined to become one of the most efficient killing machines of World War I.

B. Richardson volunteered for service with the Newcastle Commercials, and his comments on that day reveal a great deal about the determination of young men to enlist for active service in World War I:

"I tried to enlist but, after waiting for two hours, I was examined by a doctor and was rejected. My chest only measured twenty-eight inches. I went across the Tyne on the ferry and tried the recruiting office at North Shields. I found the doctor there more easily suited and he marked my chest as thirty-eight inches. I went home and told my mother but she cried, saying I was only a boy. I was eighteen."

Source: M. Middlebrook, *The First Day on the Somme*

In Great Britain many battalions were raised in local areas or from men of the same profession. These battalions had names like "3rd Manchester Pals," "Newcastle Commercials," and "Tyneside Irish." The Glasgow City Tramways Department opened a recruiting office at the trolley depot and raised a complete battalion in 16 hours! However, it would take time to turn these enthusiastic civilians into soldiers.

"Your Country Needs You:" one of the most famous recruiting posters ever produced

New recruits are taken in hand after enlisting. The British army asked for 100,000 volunteers but received 500,000 applications in just three weeks.

Early maneuvers

The first French move was an offensive into Alsace and Lorraine, which had been lost to Germany in 1871. The attacks all faltered against fire from machine guns and artillery. In these battles France suffered its heaviest casualties of the war. About 329,000 men were killed during the first two months, and the French generals blamed the soldiers. The lack of success, they said, was due to the soldiers' lack of fighting spirit!

A contemporary painting by H. Chartier, showing French troops in action in 1914. In the face of fire from machine guns and artillery, traditional charges with bayonets such as this often led to terrible casualties rather than important gains.

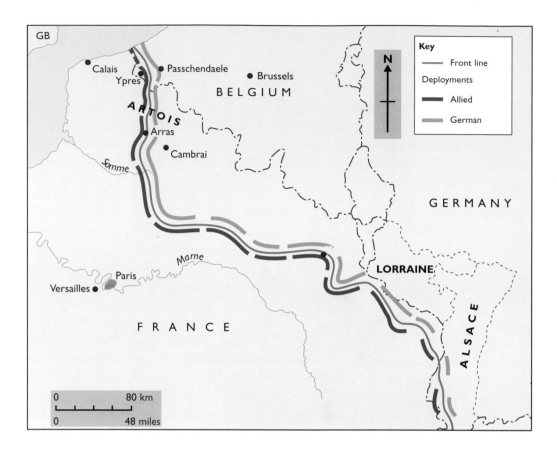

Key
Front line
Deployments
Allied
German

The Western Front, 1914.
Once it was established, the
Front hardly moved until
1918.

The German army had marched through Belgium and was now on its way toward Paris. An observation aircraft discovered and reported these moves. The French army managed to deploy and stop the Germans at the Marne. Now began a series of maneuvers as the two armies tried to get around each other's flank. This became known as the "race to the sea." At Ypres in Belgium, the German army pushed forward to gain control over the Channel ports. It was stopped by the British Expeditionary Force (BEF), but both sides suffered heavy losses. The British 7th Division went into battle with 12,300 men and emerged with only 2,400.

Soldiers now discovered what Ivan Bloch had already suggested: digging trenches was the only way to avoid the bullets. As winter set in, a continuous line of trenches stretched from the Swiss border to the coast of the English Channel. The Western Front was established.

This quote from the British Cavalry Training Manual (1907) illustrates how military leaders did not realize how effective modern weapons had become:

"The rifle, effective as it is, cannot replace the effect produced by the speed of the horse, the magnetism of the charge, and the terror of cold steel."

More nations would take part in the war. There would be fighting in the colonies, in the Middle East, and in Italy, but for the Germans, the French, the British, and, later, the Americans, the Western Front would be the major front of the war. Until 1918 it would hardly move.

Even though World War I quickly turned into a static trench war, commanders still hoped there would be a role for their prestigious cavalry, once the lines had been broken.

19

1915: Stalemate

A cover illustration from Le Petit Journal *of May 30, 1915 showing the fierce fighting at the Battle of Artois.*

Most people thought the war would be over by Christmas 1914. The generals had assumed the decisive blows would be delivered fast. Economists had described how it would be impossible for nations to sustain the war effort over a long period of time: the national economies would simply break down. They were proved sadly wrong. The generals had expected a war of movement and could not easily forget their visions of charging cavalry exploiting a break in the enemy lines. Such a break, however, failed to materialize.

The French offensive of 1915

Generally speaking, in 1915 the Germans decided to stay on the defensive at the Western Front and attack on the Eastern Front instead. The British had suffered grievously in the battles of 1914, and the new battalions of volunteers took time to train.

As a result, the French bore the brunt of the fighting and launched some offensives. One became known as the Battle of Artois. The French guns fired 2,155,862 shells over a six-day period as a preliminary bombardment. This amounts to 250 shells every minute, night and day. It was a terrifying shower of steel and explosives intended to knock a large hole in the German line.

The attackers managed to move forward almost 2.4 mi. (4 km) in just two hours. But the reserves were slow in following, and the Germans counterattacked. The French attackers discovered that the Germans had already developed very sophisticated trench systems. A sector of the front, north of Arras, known as the "Labyrinth," contained numerous underground tunnels, death traps, strongholds, and other devices aimed at killing attackers. The offensive boiled down to more than a month of hard fighting, in which 150,000 French and more than 75,000 German soldiers became casualties. No breakthrough was achieved.

The opening phase of the Battle of Artois suggested that artillery might be able to achieve important results. But 1915 was a year in which the armies lacked ammunition and heavy guns in the quantities needed for such bombardments. It took time to turn the national economies to war production. British lack of success at the Battle of Neuve Chapelle was blamed on a shortage of ammunition, which was in turn blamed on the munitions workers. This resulted in the compulsory closing of pubs in the afternoon in order to encourage men to work rather than drink— a result of World War I felt in England for decades afterward.

The industrialization of Europe during the nineteenth century created the necessary basis for the huge production of arms needed to supply the Western Front. Here shells are being produced in the north of England.

A French officer described the nightmare of fighting in the Labyrinth:

"For three weeks we were not able to get rid of the dead bodies, amongst which we used to live night and day! One burrow, a hundred and twenty feet long, took us thirteen days of ceaseless fighting to conquer entirely. The Germans had placed barricades, trapdoors, and traps of all descriptions. When we stumbled we risked being impaled on bayonets treacherously hidden in holes lightly covered with earth. And all this went on in almost complete darkness."

Source: N. Cave,
Vimy Ridge, Arras

Senegalese soldiers, fighting for France, trying on their gas masks. Gas masks were essential for survival but made it very difficult for a soldier to see what was happening during an attack.

Ferdinand Foch (1851–1929)

General Ferdinand Foch wrote books on warfare and headed the French military staff college before World War I. His strong emphasis on "fighting spirit" and "attack" rather than defense came to dominate the thinking of a generation of French officers. This led to disastrous losses in the opening months of 1914 and during the Battle of Artois in 1915. However, Foch's never-failing optimism and his belief that "A battle lost is a battle which one believes is lost" did help to stop the German advance in 1914.

Foch was relieved of command in 1916, because he seemed unable to break the deadlock. In the last year of the war, he was made supreme commander of the combined Allied forces, helped to stop the German offensive, and finally dictated the armistice terms to the Germans in November 1918.

Deadlock

Some hoped to break the trench deadlock by introducing new weapons. The Germans introduced two in 1915, both near Ypres. The first was poison gas, used for the first time on the Western Front in April 1915. It came as a shock, and the defenders were left in complete chaos for a while. However, the German attackers—although they were equipped with gas masks—were themselves reluctant to move into the greenish-yellow cloud of gas. The second new weapon was known as "liquid fire." On a July morning, at the village of Hooge, the Germans used flamethrowers to spray liquid fire over British soldiers for the first time in the war. The flamethrowers were crewed by former firemen. Both these weapons were soon copied by the British and the French, but neither helped break the deadlock.

G. V. Carey of the British 8th Rifle Brigade described the Germans' first use of flamethrowers, or liquid fire:

"I saw three or four distinct sheets of flame—like a line of powerful fire-hoses spraying fire instead of water—shoot across my fire trench. How long this lasted is impossible to say—probably not more than a minute; but the effect was so stupefying that, for my own part, I was utterly unable for some moments to think collectively."

Source: N. Cave, *Sanctuary Wood & Hooge*

Both sides undertook mining activities at some sectors of the Front in an effort to break the deadlock. Where the ground was firm, tunnels were dug under the enemy trenches and explosives were laid inside, which were then detonated. "Clay kickers" who, in peacetime, had been excavating tunnels for sewers or underground railroads, were found to be very useful for this job.

"Clay kickers" mining on the Western Front with the aim of planting explosives to blow up enemy trenches.

It was extremely nerve-racking to serve in trenches that could be blown up at any moment. Listening equipment was devised to discover enemy mining by the sounds it transmitted through the ground. This kind of warfare led to local gains. But it was a slow way to advance, and sometimes tunnels were blown up from other tunnels dug next to or beneath them.

Effectively the armies were bogged down in something that resembled siege warfare. But whereas the defenders of a medieval castle under siege were cut off from any supplies, the situation was completely different on the Western Front. The trains that had brought the soldiers to the Front continued to run. They brought in more men, weapons, ammunition, barbed wire, and everything else needed to improve the defensive positions in the trenches. Ironically, they also brought in huge amounts of fodder for the horses, because the generals kept their forces of cavalry in idle readiness, just in case. Fodder required more transportation capacity than any other item on the Western Front.

Whenever a section of the Front was threatened, the trains would swiftly move men and supplies to the sector under threat. The attackers would have to move forward across no man's land on foot. No man's land was ground between a friendly trench and an enemy trench.

Listening equipment like this, adapted from an ordinary telephone receiving apparatus, was used to try to detect enemy miners.

Daily Life in the Trenches

Once a young man had joined the army, he had very little say in what would eventually happen to him. Military discipline would be a shock, although strict discipline was less of a novelty at that time than it would be to young people today. In the early twentieth century, children were not generally encouraged to voice their opinions on any matter. When small they were expected to keep quiet and do what their parents or teachers told them. Later, as young workers or apprentices, obedience was still demanded, even though conditions in workshops and factories were smelly, noisy, and unpleasant. The noncommissioned officers (NCOs) in the military training camps built on this respect for authority and turned it into total, blind obedience, which was essential for maintaining discipline in the trenches.

The journey to the Front

Soldiers were taken by train almost all the way to the Front. Soldiers from England would first have to cross the English Channel by steamer, each ship loaded to capacity with men. Crossings would often take place at night to reduce the chance of the ships being spotted and attacked by the German submarines (U-boats). If a big battle was raging, the distant thunder of artillery could be heard from the ships and even from the south coast of England.

British troops embarking for the sea voyage to France and the Western Front. Many would never see England again.

Front-line trenches would inevitably have been a shock to newly arrived troops. Dead and severely wounded soldiers were a common sight, particularly if fighting had recently taken place. Here French soldiers try to make their way through a trench filled with wounded.

Nearer the Front new soldiers often underwent further training before marching to the trenches for the first time. On the way, they would pass damaged villages and casualty clearing stations, which would be busy treating the wounded if there had been recent fighting. They might also pass by one of the numerous airfields that were situated close behind the Front.

The trench network

Going into the trenches, the soldiers would come first to the reserve trenches, then to the line of support trenches, and finally to the front-line trench. The three lines were joined by communication trenches. This complex system of trenches was designed to make it as difficult as possible for the enemy to overrun them.

Sung infinitely to the tune of "Auld Lang Syne," this song illustrates the quiet despair felt by many soldiers in the trenches:

"We're here because we're here
Because we're here because we're here
We're here because we're here because
We're here because we're here."

No man's land. The constant pounding of artillery during the big offensives completely devastated landscapes such as this forest.

Trenches usually had names. British soldiers might walk through "The Strand" or "New Bond Street," while German soldiers might pass through "Hansa Weg" or "Münster Gasse." The sickening smell of dead bodies would hang in the air. The armies tried to bury their dead, but it was not possible to recover them all. Consequently, all along the Western Front lay the rotting bodies of dead soldiers.

Beyond the front-line trench were the barbed-wire fences and no man's land. No man's land was the cratered shell-torn ground between a friendly trench and that of the enemy. No man's land could be anything from a few to several hundred feet wide. Most days there was little, if any, fighting, and new soldiers arriving at the Front would find a landscape seemingly devoid of life except for the odd rabbit running about or larks hovering unconcerned high in the sky. Taking a closer look could be fatal, however. Some new soldiers who raised their heads above the parapet of the trench were killed instantly by carefully camouflaged enemy snipers.

Most trenches were dug deep enough so that men could walk around without being seen above the ground. On the side of the trench facing the enemy, there would be a firestep. Standing on this a soldier could aim his rifle at enemy attackers. In the bottom of the trench, there were wooden planks—called duckboards—to help keep the feet dry if the trench was muddy.

French soldiers protected by their trench, about to mount the firestep

Ordinary British soldiers were expected to sleep in the open in their trenches.

Because the Germans planned to maintain their positions for a lengthy period of time, they had the best-constructed trenches. They had deep dugouts that offered protection from almost any British or French shell. Some German trenches even had electric lights and running water. The British and French, on the other hand, intended to push the Germans back and liberate the occupied parts of France and Belgium. They regarded their trenches as only temporary, so they were much more basic. Only officers had the luxury of sleeping in covered dugouts. The regular soldiers had to spend the night in the open under waterproof sheets. British and French military leaders didn't want their men to become soft or too comfortable in the trenches. This concern also led to British soldiers not having helmets until the spring of 1916. Once helmets were issued, the number of head wounds was immediately reduced by 75 percent.

Capital punishment

Discipline in the trenches was strict. Failure to obey orders could result in severe punishment. British soldiers could be sentenced to do dirty and unpleasant jobs, after which they might be chained to the wheel of an artillery gun for two hours per day for up to 21 days. In some cases, following attacks that had been completely broken up by enemy fire, French military courts randomly selected soldiers to be shot as an example of what would happen to cowards.

During the course of World War I, 3,080 British soldiers were sentenced to death for desertion, cowardice, mutiny, or other offenses. In 346 cases the sentence was actually carried out. This equals approximately one soldier shot every five days. The German army shot 48 of its own soldiers during the war.

Capital punishment was thought by many to be unwarranted and excessively harsh.

Robert Burns served in the 7th Queen's Own Cameron Highlanders and recalled his experiences of lice in the trenches:

"The lice were terrible, making you itch as they ate you. The kilts we wore were pleated and the lice got into the pleats, hundreds of them. I don't know who thought of the idea, but when the chance arose you dug a hole in the ground about two inches deep, put the kilt in the hole and covered it over with the soil. If you left it for a couple of hours, you'd find nearly all the lice had gone."

Source: Emden & Humphries, *Veterans: The Last Survivors of the Great War*

A day at the Front

A day at the Western Front started with everybody manning the firestep in case the enemy attacked at dawn. Some days the men would fire their rifles, but as long as everybody stayed in their trenches, few were hit. Usually there was no shooting at breakfast time—by some unspoken agreement many soldiers observed a sort of truce at mealtimes. If the day was quiet—and most were—it would be spent relaxing, writing letters, mending equipment, or even sleeping. Getting rid of the lice that plagued most men was a necessary pastime, but usually a battle lost.

Two members of a Highland regiment with their "trench cat"—certainly a more agreeable companion than the rats and lice that usually kept the men company in the trenches!

All this activity took place outdoors, and on nice summer days it could be an almost acceptable experience. During other seasons it was pure cold and wet misery. On their arrival at the Front, most soldiers were in good physical shape, but the harsh living conditions combined with a lack of fresh vegetables and vitamins quickly made them prone to illness and disease. German statistics show that on average 8.6 percent of German soldiers were sick at any one time.

There was often no shortage of muddy rainwater in the trenches, but this was of little use for washing.

Keeping clean in the trenches was next to impossible. Some sectors of the Front would have waterlogged trenches, forcing the soldiers to walk ankle-deep in mud and water. Other than this, water was in short supply. Men tried to collect rainwater to wash with, but generally had no choice but to remain dirty.

In the evening a hot meal might be brought up from the support trenches. Hot food was essential for the health and good spirits of the troops, but was not always available. It had to be carried to the front-line trench. If the communication trenches were under fire, this was not possible. Food in the front-line trench therefore at times consisted only of hard biscuits and canned pork, beef, or beans.

When darkness fell, patrols were sometimes sent out across no man's land to spy on or raid the enemy trenches. The British generals believed strongly in keeping up the offensive spirit of the troops. During the course of World War I, tens of thousands of soldiers lost their lives in such minor trench raids. Other soldiers

The war in the trenches demanded a great deal of hard physical labor on the part of the troops.

Almost 100,000 Chinese worked for the British behind the lines. They were often required to work for ten hours per day seven days a week, with "due considerations" made for Chinese festivals.

might leave the trench to repair or improve their own barbed-wire fences. The ever-present rats would be more active at night, and the troops might try to ambush some before going to sleep. All night sentries would be watchfully looking across no man's land to spot any moving shadows in the dark. Hopefully the night would be as quiet as the day.

In the long run, soldiers at the Front who did not see action for weeks on end couldn't keep up any great hatred of the enemy. Men on both sides shared the same miseries and fears. A common attitude of live and let live developed in many places. Sometimes incorrect information was relayed to the artillery batteries so that their shells would not hit the enemy. The soldiers in the enemy trench were then expected to return the favor.

The war in the trenches demanded lots of hard physical labor. Soldiers not manning the front line were kept busy digging new trenches, cutting up firewood, transporting ammunition, or whatever else was needed. The demand for manual labor was so great that the British army hired men from as far away as China to work behind the lines.

A "Rose of no man's land" and her patient in a hospital behind the lines. Only a very few soldiers were lucky enough to make it this far if they were seriously wounded. Most died in no man's land or in casualty clearing stations near the front line.

The roses of no man's land

Many women served as nurses in World War I, either in hospitals at home or in casualty clearing stations close to the front line. Some 100,000 civilian German women helped take care of dying and wounded soldiers. Later in the war the U.S. army would employ 20,000 nurses, of whom 25 percent served on the Western Front. In Great Britain there were 18,000 military nurses and, by 1918, over 80,000 civilian female volunteers. About 8,000 of these worked near the Front, often close enough to risk being shelled.

Theoretically these women should have been at least 23 years old to work on the Western Front, but many as young as 17 were accepted because the demand for nurses was so high. They became known as "The roses of no man's land" for their dedication, compassion, and hard work.

After a period of perhaps ten days, a unit manning the front-line trench would be relieved and walk back behind the lines. Here there would be no fear of raids at night and less risk of artillery bombardment. Behind the Front, soldiers would get a chance to wash. Genuine attempts were made to provide facilities for this, although in some cases up to 100 men would have to use the same barrel of disinfected water. Leave was granted but was not generous: in the British army a soldier could expect about ten days' leave every 15 months.

In 1916 two major offensives took place, resulting in the Battle of Verdun and the Battle of the Somme. Artillery was a key weapon in both battles, and an artillery "barrage" was greatly feared by the men in the trenches. The trenches gave no real protection from the devastating effects of artillery shells. They could kill by the blast of the explosion, which might blow a man to tiny pieces. If a heavy shell landed close to a trench, the explosion might collapse it, burying alive any soldiers trying to find cover at the bottom.

With varying degrees of success, artillery played a key role in the battles of 1916.

More often, a shell would kill or maim as a result of the fragments, or shrapnel, it threw out when it exploded. The metal casing would turn into a shower of burning-hot irregular-shaped pieces of metal. Shell fragments tore into bodies in the most frightful ways, cutting off arms, legs, or heads. The fragments might also cut open the stomach, causing the intestines to spill out onto the duckboards at the bottom of the trench.

Mortars and some guns fired shells with a high trajectory. Mortar bombs in particular could be seen and followed in flight. This gave soldiers a short time in which to guess where a shell would land and run around a corner of the trench, hopefully saving their lives. Other guns shot projectiles with a flat trajectory. These were less likely to fall into the trench, but would arrive with next to no warning—like a train passing your own in the opposite direction. Whether he was watching larks, writing letters home, eating his lunch, or fixing his bayonet prior to an attack, a soldier in the trenches could never be sure that a shell would not arrive within the next few seconds. Sixty percent of all casualties on the Western Front were caused by artillery.

The Battle of Verdun

In 1916 the generals on both sides laid plans that rested heavily on artillery. The German general staff focused their plans on the French salient around Verdun. The French lines would have been much easier to defend without the salient. But, unlike the Germans and British, the French were fighting on their own soil. The strong nationalist feelings of the times dictated that not

Shrapnel from shells was deadly. This soldier was amazingly lucky that his helmet took most of the impact.

another piece of French ground would be surrendered —even if this meant leaving the army in a weak defensive position. The Germans realized this and assumed, correctly, that the French would defend Verdun at all costs.

The defense of Fort Vaux

The fight for Fort Vaux illustrates the stubbornness with which the French fought at Verdun. A small garrison held out for several days even when the Germans had begun to enter the fort. The defenders were subjected to attacks by gas and flamethrowers. Their water supply was running out. They had no food and found it impossible to sleep. When it became clear that no French support would save them, their commander had these thoughts:

"Had I the right to prolong resistance beyond human strength and to compromise uselessly the lives of these brave men who had done their duty so heroically? I took a turn in the corridors. What I saw was frightening. Men were overcome with vomiting due to urine in the stomach, for so wretched were they that they had reached the point of drinking their own urine. Some lost consciousness."

He surrendered the next day. The surviving defenders shouted *"Vive la France!"* before becoming prisoners.

French soldiers held out in forts such as Fort Vaux and Fort de Douaumont (seen here), which still stands today.

Verdun was close to the German border, making it easy for the Germans to bring in troops and ammunition by rail. The German attack was intended to include only limited assaults by infantry. The big killer was artillery, which fired from all directions into the salient, killing the French soldiers in large numbers. The Germans then expected the French to bring in reinforcements to fill the gaps, and then these troops would also be killed. In short, the German general staff hoped the French army would bleed to death at Verdun.

"La Ravin de la Mort Verdun" *by Joseph Gueldry:* The Valley of Death, Verdun.

Henri-Philippe Pétain (1856–1951)

Marshal Henri-Philippe Pétain (left, with General Foch) gained fame at Verdun. During 1914–15, he did much to improve the tactics of the French army. He became a national hero for his successful defense at Verdun. By relying heavily on artillery, he tried to avoid the excessive losses that the French army suffered early in the war. He was criticized by General Foch and others for this cautious approach. Between the wars Pétain influenced the design of the defensive Maginot Line. During World War II, he collaborated with the Germans and helped them take action against French Jews. He was tried after the war and condemned to death, but this was changed to life imprisonment. His wish to be buried among the fallen of Verdun was not granted.

The Germans opened their attack just after 7:00 A.M. on February 21. About 1,200 guns pounded the French trenches in a bombardment heavier than anything before experienced in world history. When the German infantry went forward, they found to their surprise that some defenders had survived, and these men fought back fiercely. Some French soldiers held out in old forts that could withstand much bombardment, but otherwise had only limited military value. As predicted, the French poured more and more men into the salient in their attempt to defend it.

The attack was not as successful or as swift as the German commanders had hoped. When days turned to weeks, they changed their priorities. Their objective became not just killing French soldiers but actually taking Verdun. They would have been better off not trying to do this, just as the French would have been better off not trying to defend the town. German losses mounted as hundreds of thousands of soldiers were sent forward to take Verdun. In July the Germans called off the offensive, and the French attacked. The battle continued until December. At its end, neither army had gained or lost any significant ground.

The town of Verdun was devastated by the German attempts to take it and the French efforts to defend it. Neither side made any significant gains.

The Battle of the Somme

The French warned that their line at Verdun might not hold beyond June. To take the pressure off the Verdun front, the British army, assisted by the French, attacked on a 18-mi. (29-km) front around the Somme River. Here the British army had taken over a sector of the Western Front from the French in late 1915 and early 1916. In many ways the Somme area had been a pleasant surprise for the British, coming from the wet lowlands of Flanders. The Somme region was chalkland with rolling hills and dry trenches. Not least, it was a quiet sector where shelling before breakfast was a rarity.

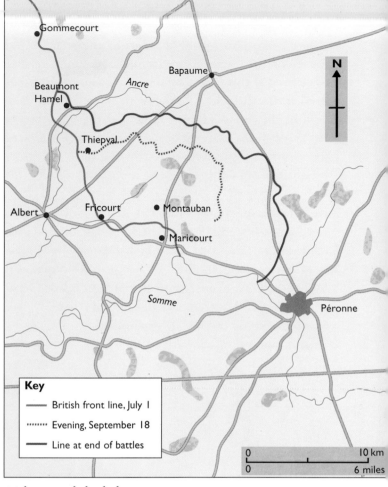

Key

—— British front line, July 1

········ Evening, September 18

—— Line at end of battles

| 0 | 10 km |
| 0 | 6 miles |

The Battle of the Somme

In early 1916 the French and British generals had chosen the Somme for an offensive. There the two armies could support each other. However, the German attack at Verdun changed the situation. Clearly the British would have to bear the main burden at the Somme, and the attack would have to be made sooner than planned. However, the British had high hopes for 1916, not least because a new army of volunteers was beginning to arrive in France from England.

As had been the case with the Germans' plan at Verdun, the British plan at the Somme relied on artillery to win the battle. When a large gap was created in the German line, cavalry would support the infantry, break through into open country in the German rear, and "roll up" the German line.

39

A seven-day bombardment preceded the attack. There was a gun for every 53 ft. (16 m) of Front. More shells were fired at this time than the total of number of shells fired in the first 12 months of the war. However, the type of shell used was not suited for the main task: to cut through the dreaded barbed-wire fences in front of the German trenches and destroy the deep dugouts in which their infantry sheltered.

Early in the morning of July 1, 120,000 British soldiers were anxiously waiting in their trenches. The divisions ready to attack on that morning had largely been raised in Ulster, London, and the industrial North and Midlands. Each man carried more than 66 lbs. (30 kg) of equipment. The soldiers had been told that no Germans would be alive. It would be a cinch, and consequently they

Ten mines were detonated beneath the German lines before the attack on the Somme began on July 1. The largest mine had been filled with 18 tons of explosives, producing this huge eruption of earth.

British soldiers prior to the main offensive at the Somme. They had been told the attack would be an easy one.

should form long lines and proceed at a steady walking pace toward the supposedly smashed German trenches. The generals assumed that this inexperienced new army of civilian volunteers would not be capable of using more advanced tactics such as rushing up to the enemy trenches.

At 7:30 A.M. the artillery barrage lifted, the officers blew their whistles, and the men went over the top. Immediately, the killing started. The shelling had been a terrible ordeal for the Germans, but the majority were still alive, and the barbed wire was intact along long stretches of the front line. German machine guns and artillery cut down wave after wave of attackers. Many British soldiers only managed to get a few feet from their own trenches before they were hit.

The French offensive fared better than the British, although neither army managed to break through the German line.

A detailed breakdown of the British casualties on the first day of the Somme reveals how the regular infantry suffered by far the most casualties:

Type of unit	Casualties
Regular infantry	54,335
Machine gun companies	1,080
Pioneer battalions	1,020
Royal Engineers	450
Light trench mortar batteries	350
Artillery	170
Royal Army Medical Corps	60
Royal Flying Corps	5

The two great Western Front battles of 1916 both dragged on for months and produced casualties on a scale never experienced before in war:

Casualties by nationality

	British	French	German
Verdun	–	315,000	281,000
Somme	420,000	200,000	450,000

Some British gains were made, especially on the southern part of the front. In most places, however, the British made no advances on the first day.

When the sun set over the battlefield, the British army had suffered almost 60,000 casualties—40,000 wounded and 20,000 dead. The medical units were totally overwhelmed because the planning had "only" calculated the need to transport 10,000 wounded per day. However, there were not even enough ambulance trains to cater for this number. Many wounded died in the congested casualty clearing stations immediately behind the Front. In no man's land some wounded survived for days, drinking muddy water from the bottom of shell holes before they lost consciousness or managed to crawl back into their own trenches.

A sergeant in the 3rd Tyneside Irish described the experience of leading his men across no man's land in the face of the German machine gun fire:

"I could see, away to my left and right, long lines of men. Then I heard the 'patter, patter' of machine guns in the distance. By the time I'd gone another ten yards there seemed to be only a few men left around me; by the time I had gone twenty yards I seemed to be on my own. Then I was hit myself."

Source: J. Keegan, *The Face of Battle*

British troops go over the top at the Somme.

The first day of the Somme was a disaster at home in England as well as on the field of battle. Because of the local nature of the volunteer units, some British communities found themselves deprived of their whole populations of young men: husbands, fathers and sons—wage-earners all wiped out in a single day on the fields of France. Despite this, the attack had to continue in order to support the French at Verdun. The battle raged for 140 days.

British soldiers near Beaumont Hamel in November, 1916

Norman Collins, a young officer of the Scottish 51st Highland Division, took part in burying dead soldiers after the capture of Beaumont Hamel in November 1916:

"I was told to go back into what had been no man's land and bury the old dead killed on 1st July. The flesh had gone mainly from the faces but the hair had still grown, the beards to some extent. They looked very ragged, very ragged and the rats were running out of their chests. To a rat it was just a nest, but to think that a human being provided a nest for a rat was a pretty dreadful feeling. For a young fellow like myself, nineteen, all I had to look forward to at the time was a similar fate."

Source: Emden & Humphries,
Veterans: The Last Survivors of the Great War

1917: Attrition

The year 1917 was one of great changes in world history. At the beginning of the year, the old European powers were fighting a war as they had so often done before, albeit on a far larger scale. At the end of 1917, Russia was in chaos because of revolutionary turmoil and had dropped out of the war. Germany had tried to starve Great Britain of supplies through a campaign of unrestricted U-boat warfare. This led to the sinking of many ships. Earlier in 1915, the British liner *Lusitania* had been sunk by a U-boat attack. More than 1,195 civilians were lost, including 128 American passengers. The United States was starting to look at Europe's problems seriously. The U-boat campaign failed, but not before it had sufficiently enraged the United States to declare war on Germany. It would take time, however, for American soldiers to reach the Western Front.

For the men in the trenches, 1917 was just another year of soldiering. The munitions factories continued to produce weapons and ammunition, in order to ensure that the men at the Front were in no danger of lacking the means to kill the enemy.

The race for new weapons

As we have seen, the generals of World War I were willing to accept huge casualties. However, it would be wrong to assume that nothing was done to find ways of trying to break the trench deadlock. The inventiveness that had led to the industrialization of Europe was now spent developing and producing arms.

Germany made great use of U-boats against merchant as well as military shipping during World War I.

British no.1 Squadron, ready for action on the Western Front. Although flying was often perceived as a glamorous occupation, pilots had an extremely short life expectancy.

The air war

During World War I, airplanes became an essential element in warfare for the first time. Their main function was to observe and photograph enemy trenches and troop movements. They also helped direct artillery fire. Some would drop bombs, but planes at that time were able to carry only small loads. To deny the enemy the advantages of air observation, fighters were developed to shoot their planes down. Great "dogfights" were fought high over the trenches. The best fighter pilots became known as aces and achieved great·fame. The press likened them to medieval knights fighting duels, which was much more romantic than telling people about the mass killing in the trenches. However, there was nothing romantic about the air war. Pilots flew without parachutes, and many survived only a few weeks at the Front before being killed.

In his book *Sagittarius Rising*, Cecil Lewis, a pilot in the British Royal Flying Corps, described how the war was put into stark perspective when viewed from the air:

"The war below us was a spectacle. We aided and abetted it, admiring the tenacity of men who fought in filth to take the next trench thirty yards away. The fearful thing about the war became its horrible futility, the mountainous waste of life and wealth to stake a mile or two of earth. There was so much beyond. Viewed with detachment, it had all the elements of a grotesque comedy——a fantastic caricature of common sense."

Before the war, military training had emphasized the use of rifles, but in the trenches these were found to be of little use. Many soldiers never actually shot an enemy, and it was difficult to use the bayonet in the narrow trenches. As a result, hand grenades (often called "bombs" at that time) and mortars were the most important weapons developed. Thrown grenades had been known for centuries, but they became weapons of great importance in the trenches. At first, grenades almost presented a greater hazard to the thrower than to the intended target, but they became far more reliable as the war continued. Grenades were also fired from adapted rifles or thrown by catapults.

Hand grenades were vital weapons in trench warfare.

Armament production 1914–17

	1914	1915	1916	1917
Machine guns				
Great Britain	300	6,100	33,500	79,700
Germany	2,400	6,100	27,600	115,200
Explosives (tons)				
Great Britain	5,000	24,000	76,000	186,000
Germany	14,400	72,000	120,000	144,000

Source: N. Ferguson, *The Pity of War*

Mortars were simple weapons compared to guns, but were extremely effective. By 1917, soldiers equipped with mortars could knock out machine gun posts like those responsible for the death of so many British soldiers attacking at the Somme. Other mortars fired drums of gas. Some 2,000 of these were set up for the attack on Vimy Ridge north of Arras in April 1917.

Vimy Ridge

In many places along the Western Front, the Germans had wisely dug their trenches on high ground. This gave them good views of the enemy trenches below. Vimy Ridge was just such a strongly defended area. In April it was attacked by Canadian divisions of the British army, working together for the first time as a purely Canadian force. The attack was well planned, and all preparations had been efficiently carried out.

About 21 mi. (34 km) of signaling cable were buried over 6.5 ft. (2 m) deep to protect them from heavy shelling. About 50,000 horses were brought in to pull the wagons moving supplies.

Eleven trainloads of building materials arrived daily to be used for repair and maintenance of the roads in the area. The ammunition dumps were stocked with 42,500 tons of artillery shells.

The attack opened with a massive artillery bombardment. Bursting gas drums produced a high concentration of gas that killed many of the Germans in the deep dugouts. The Canadian force was 35,000 strong, and although enough Germans survived to cause the Canadians 10,000 casualties, the ridge was finally taken. In the context of the trench war, this was considered a success. Small steps forward became great victories.

However, there was no real breakthrough because the Germans brought up their reserves. The plan had called for the offensive to be stopped if serious resistance was encountered. In spite of this, the British commander-in-chief, General Haig, maintained the attack on a wider front even though the Germans were fighting back. Little progress was made, but 148,000 more casualties were inflicted on the Allies.

Vimy Ridge and the ensuing unsuccessful attempts to break the German line demonstrated that even improved weapons and carefully implemented tactics could not overcome the basic problem of the trench war: defenders could always bring in reinforcements more quickly by rail than attackers could move forward on foot.

Sir Douglas Haig (1861–1928)

In December 1915 Sir Douglas Haig was commander-in-chief of the British army on the Western Front. Haig had distinguished himself in colonial wars in Africa as a cavalry officer. He was a man slow to accept new ideas. When machine guns were first used in the army, he claimed that "bullets had little stopping power against a horse." In World War I, Haig believed in keeping up the "offensive spirit" and wearing down the German army through a process of attrition.

The huge casualties required to achieve the Allied victory in 1918 made Haig a controversial figure after the war. He saw no other option than to accept casualties as the price of victory, but contrary to popular opinion, he was not indifferent to the suffering of his troops. When Sir William Orphen arrived at Haig's headquarters to paint his portrait in 1917, Haig told him: "Why waste your time painting me? Go and paint the men. They're the fellows who are saving the world, and they're getting killed every day."

Mutiny

The Allied attack in April 1917 had been partly in support of a French offensive at Chemin des Dames. There the French general, Robert-Georges Nivelle, expected to be able to break through the German lines. But when the artillery barrage ceased, the Germans had already withdrawn some distance to a carefully prepared system of trenches known as the Hindenburg line. The French soldiers were pushed on, but heavy casualties caused widespread mutiny.

Men simply refused to go over the top. They were prepared to defend France, but they were no longer willing to take part in more futile attacks. The trench war had drained away the offensive spirit of the French army. As a result, the war on the Western Front increasingly became a conflict between Germany and Great Britain.

Between April and May 1917, there was widespread mutiny in the French army. This cartoon from the time shows an officer trying to inspire his troops, who are clearly less than enthusiastic about what he is saying.

Passchendaele

The "Third Battle of Ypres"—a battle better known as Passchendaele after a completely obliterated village taken in its last phase—was the major British attempt of 1917 to break through the German lines. The battle has the doubtful honor of being regarded as perhaps the most tragic trench battle of World War I.

At Ypres the British army planned to attack from a salient it had held for most of the war. As at Vimy Ridge, the Germans had the advantage of overlooking the British trenches in the reclaimed bogland below. The British crammed nearly one million men into the salient prior to the attack. The Germans reinforced their position with the same number of men. In late July the heaviest artillery bombardment so far attempted fell on the German lines. More than four million shells weighing a total of 107,000 tons were fired. German guns returned the fire, trying to kill soldiers moving up to the lines and destroying British guns.

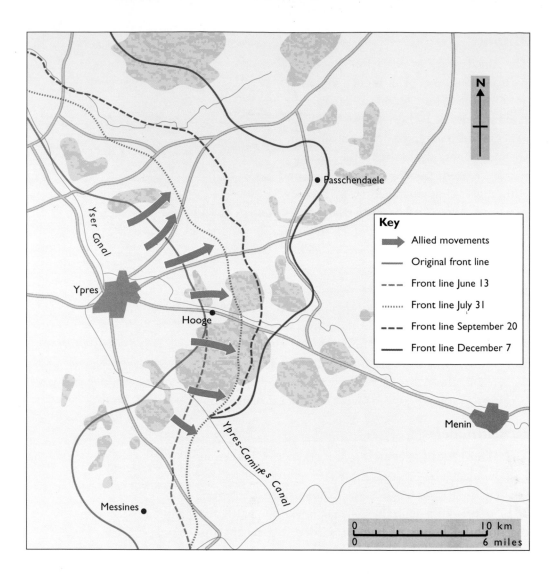

Key

➤ Allied movements

— Original front line

--- Front line June 13

.... Front line July 31

--- Front line September 20

— Front line December 7

The shells completely devastated the area. Drainage systems were destroyed, and, as heavy rain set in, the battlefield turned into a sea of mud. The artillery had created an impossible situation for the attack, which nonetheless took place as planned. Soaked through, the British soldiers walked up to the lines on slimy duckboards. Many slipped and literally drowned in the mud. It became impossible to move any heavy guns. The attackers moved forward only with difficulty and were easily cut down by the defenders. Casualty evacuation broke down. Horse-drawn ambulances skidded and crashed.

The Third Battle of Ypres, also known as Passchendaele

For a terrified young soldier, there was no easy way out of the horror. Turning back would be "desertion" or "cowardice," for which he could be shot. Numb with fear, men gathered in the remnants of the front-line trenches and went forward as ordered. A soldier who was wounded badly enough to be sent back home to England, but not badly enough to be permanently disabled, was considered lucky.

During the course of the battle, ruined villages and trenches changed hands several times. Hand-to-hand combat was brutal, because everyone killed to survive. Rifle butts and spades were used to smash skulls or faces. Fights with hand grenades raged from one shell hole to the next. Such events were common to all the major battles of World War I, but Passchendaele, "the battle of the mud," was especially trying as it was clear to the vast majority of front-line soldiers that there would be no breakthrough. It was just another horrendous battle of attrition in which they were being killed in the hope that the enemy soldiers would be killed at a faster rate.

The horrors of "going over the top" and running toward an enemy trench are vividly described in the book *All Quiet on the Western Front* by Erich Maria Remarque. He himself fought in the German army during World War I:

"We have lost all feelings for others, we barely recognize each other when somebody comes into our line of vision, agitated as we are. We are dead men with no feelings, who are able by some trick, some dangerous magic, to keep on running and keep on killing ... for a second or so we duck down behind a parapet ... we toss explosives into the dugouts; the earth shakes, creaking, smoking and groaning, we stumble over slippery fragments of flesh, over soft bodies; I fall into a belly that has been ripped open, and on the body is a new, clean, French officer's cap."

Heavy rain turned the shell-torn lowlands of the Ypres battlefield into a sea of mud.

The psychological toll

Some men couldn't stand the prolonged mental strains of trench warfare. An Australian officer once found 50 Manchester men taking cover amidst piles of dead and moaning wounded. He later commented that "Never have I seen men so broken and demoralized in the last stages of exhaustion and fear." Some soldiers in the trenches literally went crazy, while others became so mentally disturbed that they couldn't control body movements or emotional reactions.

The term "shell shock" was used to describe the condition when a man was utterly unable to continue. Psychiatry became a part of military medicine. After the war, 65,000 British ex-servicemen received disability pensions because of mental problems. Many never recovered sufficiently to leave the psychiatric hospitals.

When the battle ended in November 1917, Haig claimed it "had served its purpose." During the battle the purpose was conveniently changed from "breaking through" to "killing Germans." Men had certainly been killed: British casualties amounted to over 250,000. The Germans had lost around 200,000 men. After the battle, a senior British officer

Soldiers such as this private were treated for shell shock so that they could return to the Front as quickly as possible.

was for the first time driven out to the muddy battlefield in a car. As the going became more and more difficult, he finally burst into tears, muttering "Good God, did we really send men out to fight in that?" Another passenger, who knew the battlefield well, replied, "It's worse further up."

The battlefield at Ypres. It was impossible for men to fight effectively in such conditions.

The tank offensive

Tanks were first developed in great secrecy in the English city of Lincoln in 1915. British officers had suggested that an armored fighting vehicle would perhaps be able to break through the enemy lines. Various cover names were given to the new device. One was "water carrier" but this was soon changed to "tank." A few tanks were used at the Somme, but they first became available in great numbers during 1917. Some were used at Passchendaele, where they became hopelessly stuck in the mud.

The Tank Corps suggested that tanks should instead be used farther south at Cambrai. There, on firm ground without shell holes and with no preliminary bombardment, nearly 400 tanks went forward in massed formation. The attack took the Germans completely by surprise. Tanks and infantry went forward 5 mi. (8 km), overrunning all three German lines. The British suffered 1,500 casualties and lost a number of tanks due to German fire and mechanical breakdowns, but managed to take 10,000 Germans prisoner. However, the British army had spent all its reserves at Passchendaele, and it was not able to exploit the success at Cambrai. Once again the Germans

A tank in action. If they did not get stuck in the mud, early tanks like this proved an effective weapon.

counterattacked, the lines thickened, and the soldiers could look forward only to another bleak winter in their trenches.

The perils of surrender

It could be dangerous to surrender on the Western Front. In the chaos of close combat, most soldiers would kill a surrendering enemy if they were in the slightest

doubt about his real intentions. Some would kill him regardless. If a man had just seen several of his friends being killed, he might see no reason why their killers should live. However, between 6 and 8.5 million men were taken prisoner during the course of World War I. Prisoners became important to the war economies because they were used to do the work that a nation's own young men could not do because they were serving in the trenches. In Germany, 900,000 Russians worked in agriculture. More than 190,000 British soldiers were taken prisoner, many of whom worked in German stone quarries and coal mines.

A German officer surrenders and is taken prisoner by two American soldiers. U.S. troops started arriving in Europe in large numbers in the summer of 1918.

1918: New Tactics

At first glance the prospects for 1918 didn't look bright for the Allies. Morale was low and victory nowhere in sight. The British divisions on the Western Front were 150,000 men under strength. In Great Britain, 645,000 trained soldiers were waiting, but Prime Minister David Lloyd George held them back from France. He feared that Haig would just waste them in more futile "decisive" offensives if given the chance to do so.

Industrial production in Great Britain was down to 87 percent of the 1914 level. Consumption of meat was down to 25 percent. All over the country families grieved over the loss of sons and husbands. In Germany, the situation was even worse. German industrial production was down to 69 percent of prewar output. A naval blockade had cut off German imports of fertilizer. As a result, grain production dropped to 50 percent of the prewar level. Germany suffered a severe food shortage affecting both civilians and soldiers.

A cool appraisal of the situation should have made it clear that Germany could no longer win the war. Some German politicians realized this and were willing to accept a peace agreement. But the German war was run by the military general staff, not by politicians. In the minds of the military, Germany might still win after all.

The *Kaiserschlacht*

The German general Erich Ludendorff assumed that by using better tactics his army would be able to break through the British lines on the Somme front. In early 1918 the Germans transferred large numbers of troops from the East where Russia was no longer fighting. The *Kaiserschlacht* (Kaiser's Battle) opened on March 21 with a very heavy, but short, artillery bombardment. Elite storm troopers led the attack. Armed with light machine guns, they bypassed strongholds and broke through at weak points in the British line. They were helped by thick fog that made it difficult for the British artillery and machine gunners to spot them. Success seemed assured.

British prime minister David Lloyd George was reluctant to commit more troops to the Western Front during the winter of 1917–18, fearing that they would be wiped out in further offensives. He did not, however, order that Haig be replaced as commander-in-chief.

Erich Ludendorff (1865–1937)
Paul von Hindenburg (1847–1934)

During World War I, the German generals Ludendorff (on the right of the picture) and Hindenburg (on the left) formed a team that led the army and organized the home-front war effort. They had more influence on German politics than either the Kaiser or the German parliament. Hindenburg became a symbol of the German will to fight. Ludendorff was a brilliant tactician and led the development of the novel tactics that broke the British lines in 1918. Unfortunately for Germany, neither Hindenburg nor Ludendorff grasped the strategic reality that Germany did not have the resources to win the war of attrition. The unrestricted U-boat warfare and the 1918 March offensive were both gambles that did more damage to Germany than to its enemies.

Everywhere there was confusion in the British lines. Thousands surrendered when they discovered that the storm troopers were already at their rear. Over the following days the German army advanced 37 mi. (60 km) on a broad front. It had done what no other army had been able to do during the years of trench warfare.

However, the new tactics could not make up for the basic problems of supplying and reinforcing an attack on the Western Front. Enough British soldiers fought back to cause heavy German casualties. German soldiers were shocked to see how well supplied their enemies were when they looted British depots. The German advance lost its momentum. Over the following months, the Germans suffered one million casualties—a number that it was impossible to replace.

American recruits enlisting at Camp Travis, in Texas. The inexperienced U.S. army at first suffered heavy casualties when going into action against the experienced Germans. However, their arrival in Europe in 1918 gave a huge boost to the morale of the Allied troops, and eventually helped tip the balance of the war in the Allies' favor.

Out of the trenches

After the failure of the *Kaiserschlacht,* the Allies succeeded in forcing the Germans back. The effects of a naval blockade, war on two fronts, and the losses suffered during the years of attrition had seriously weakened the German army. By the summer of 1918, U.S. troops were arriving in France at the rate of 300,000 a month. The sheer weight of numbers alone served to further demoralize the German troops.

German and British casualties, March 21, 1918: the first day of the *Kaiserschlacht*

	Killed	Wounded	Prisoners	Total
German	10,851	28,778	300	39,929
British	7,512	10,000	21,000	38,512

Source: M. Middlebrook, *The Kaiser's Battle*

Not all Americans in France were combat troops. In June 1918, 25,400 U.S. troops arrived to service and repair the French railroad network so that it could support the increased flow of men and equipment.

Due to their inexperience, the Americans suffered serious casualties in their early battles against the German army. However, they displayed great courage and a willingness to press on in the face of heavy losses. The Battle of Belleau Wood in June 1918 was their first major engagement; the U.S. Marines suffered 5,000 casualties from a force of 10,000 men. Despite this, victory was achieved and provided a huge boost to Allied morale. One Frenchman described how "new life" had come "to bring a fresh, surging vigor to the body of France, bled almost to death."

A combination of fresh troops and new tactics proved to be decisive. In the fall of 1918, the German army came close to suffering a major military defeat. The Germans decided that they had no option but to agree to an armistice—an end to the fighting—while their lines still held. On November 11, 1918, the guns along the Western Front fell silent, and the war was over.

A contemporary painting showing U.S. troops in action at Belleau Wood in June 1918

The 15,000 war graves at Douaumont just outside Verdun represent just a small fraction of the many who died on the Western Front. The "Hall of Bones," which extends from the tower on each side, contains the incomplete remains of thousands of unidentified dead recovered from the battlefield.

Date List

1912 Balkan states victorious over the Ottoman Empire.

1914

June 28 Assassination of Archduke Franz Ferdinand at Sarajevo in Bosnia. Austria-Hungary holds Serbia responsible.

July 28 Austria-Hungary declares war on Serbia.

August 1 Germany declares war on Russia.

August 3 Germany declares war on France and invades Belgium.

August 4 Britain declares war on Germany. Germans advance on Paris.

August 14 French army attacks German front in western France.

August 26–30 Russian defeat by Germany at Tannenberg.

September 6–16 German advance is stopped by the French army at the Battle of the Marne.

October 10–November 10 "The race to the sea:" German and Anglo-French forces attempt to outflank each other. The Western Front is established as a result.

November 5 The Allies declare war on Turkey.

1915

February 4 Germany declares an "area of war" to exist in the waters around Great Britain and threatens to sink any ship sailing in them.

April 22 The German army uses poison gas for the first time near Ypres.

May 7 The *Lusitania* is torpedoed off the Irish coast.

May 9 French army launches an attack at Artois.

July 30 Germans use flamethrowers for the first time.

December 19 Sir Douglas Haig becomes commander-in-chief of the British army in France.

1916

February 21 Germany launches Verdun offensive.

June 24 Bombardment of German line at the Somme.

July 1 British soldiers go over the top at the Somme.

September 15 Tanks are used for the first time in battle.

November 16 Battle of the Somme ends.

December 15 Battle of Verdun ends.

Glossary

1917

March 17	Czar Nicholas II of Russia abdicates.
April 6	The United States declares war on Germany.
April 9–12	Canadian forces take Vimy Ridge.
April 16	French offensive at Chemin des Dames.
May–June	Mutinies in the French army.
July 31	British army launches an offensive at Ypres.
November 6	Bolsheviks seize power in Russia.
November 10	Third Battle of Ypres ends when the village of Passchendaele is taken.
November 20	British tanks secure success at the Battle of Cambrai.
December 17	Russia signs German armistice terms.

1918

March 21	German army launches the "Kaiser's Battle."
August 8	Highly successful British attacks make this day "the black day of the German army."
November 11	Armistice signed between the Allies and Germany.

armistice truce, especially a permanent truce. The word comes from the Latin *arma* (arms) and *sisto* (make stand).

attrition gradual wearing down.

Balkans an area in southeast Europe consisting of present-day Greece, Albania, Yugoslavia, Bulgaria, part of Romania, and the European part of Turkey.

barrage a concentrated artillery bombardment.

battalion a military unit consisting of 36 officers and 1,000 men, of whom 800 men would be combat troops.

British Expeditionary Force (BEF) the units of the British army sent to fight in France and Belgium on the Western Front in World War I.

cavalry military units using horses for transport. Traditionally the role of the cavalry was to scout for the army. On the Western Front this role was largely taken over by aircraft.

clay kicker soldier given the job of digging mine tunnels under enemy trenches.

conscription the summoning of people for compulsory service to the state, usually military service.

deadlock a state of unresolved conflict.

deploy spread out troops ready for action.

dogfight close combat between fighter aircraft.

duckboard path of wooden slats over muddy ground in a trench.

enlist enroll voluntarily in the armed services.

Flanders a historic region in Europe that now comprises the provinces of East Flanders and West Flanders in Belgium and parts of northern France and the Netherlands.

flank right or left side of an army.

general staff the group of officers commanding an army.

mortar a short-barreled muzzle-loading artillery weapon with a high-angled trajectory. Mortars are used to fire explosives and smoke bombs.

nationalism patriotic feelings or principles, often used as a policy of national independence.

Ottoman Empire a Turkish Muslim empire ruling large parts of the Middle East as well as territories in Europe from the fourteenth to the twentieth centuries.

parapet low wall in front of a trench. On the Western Front parapets could be built quite high when muddy ground prevented trenches from being dug deep enough for soldiers to take cover in them.

pioneer battalion a battalion that carried out construction work in the trenches.

salient in military terms, an area where the front line bulges out into enemy-held territory.

shrapnel this term, describing the fragments of an exploded bomb, derives from the name of the inventor of the explosive shell: Shrapnel.

Somme a river in northern France, rising in the Aisne department and flowing mainly west through Amiens and Abbeville to the English Channel. It was the scene of extensive fighting in World War I.

storm trooper an elite German soldier trained to advance fast and seize his objective.

trajectory path of an object (such as a shell) moving under the force of gunfire.

Ypres a town in western Belgium, on the Yperlee River. Its many medieval buildings were almost completely destroyed during World War I.

Resources

Sources

Books to read

Brown, Gene. *Conflict in Europe and the Great Depression: World War I (1914–1940)*. Twenty First Century, 1995.

Dolan, Edward F. *America in World War I*. Millbrook, 1996.

Hoehling, A. A. *The Last Voyage of the Lusitania*. Madison Books, 1996.

Lowry, Bullitt. *Armistice 1918*. Kent State University Press, 1997.

Ross, Stewart. *World War I: Causes and Consequences*. Raintree Steck-Vaughn, 1998.

Wilder, Amos N. *Armageddon Revisited: A World War I Journal*. Yale University Press, 1994.

Brennan, Gerald. *A Life of One's Own ....* Eyre & Spottiswoode, 1962.

Brown, Malcolm. *The Imperial War Museum Book of 1918: Year of Victory*. Sidgwick and Jackson, 1998.

Cave, Nigel. *Sanctuary Wood & Hooge*. Combined Books, 1997.

Cave, Nigel. *Vimy Ridge, Arras*. Combined Books, 1997.

Ferguson, Niall. *The Pity of War*. Basic Books, 2000.

Gilbert, Martin. *First World War*. Henry Holt, 1996.

Middlebrook, Martin. *The Kaiser's Battle*. Penguin Books, 1999.

Saunders, Anthony. *Weapons of the Trench War*. Sutton Publishing, 1999.

Taylor, A.J.P. *The Struggle for Mastery in Europe 1848–1918*. Oxford University Press, 1980.

Index

If a number is in **bold** type, there is a photo or illustration.